SUNLIGHT AND SHADOWS

————————————

a book of poetry by K. Lewis

Blue Vagabond Productions

Denver Colorado

First Edition April 2008

Copyright K. Lewis

ISBN 978-0-6152-0651-6

Dedication

I dedicate this book of poetry to my mother and father, both unknowing poets, with love. Both claim not to be poets, but my father sees with a poetic eye and my mother writes me treasured letters capturing vivid images of life.

Introduction

These poems primarily come from the two-year time period 2006 to 2007, a transitional time period of my life. At the beginning of this time period I wrote Fifty and Change which is not published as of this date. I have written many more poems, but these are representative of the time period. "Heroes," which is included, represents another transition. I have listened to many poets since 2006 and read most of these poems to others. Life has changed as well, so it is not surprising the nature of my poetry has changed. Some of these poems were written in the middle of the night, others scribbled in notes while riding in a cab, some in 3 minutes and others over days. I do not know when or where or why the muse appears to dictate the words. The title piece which concludes this book was written some years ago in a journal.

April 21, 2008   K. Lewis

Copyright 2008 Kurt Lewis All Rights Reserved

Street Sweeper

Take the fabric from the day
Fold it,
Cut it,
Sew it down the side,
Match color and sound,
Up down and around,
Swish the grit from the teeth
Flavor sometimes aint sweet
And ya have
Poetry from the street.
I stay awake all night
When the beat
Of my feet
Matches the train
Runnin in my brain
So sometimes the colors
Don't match just right
Street sweeper that's me
Cleanin dirty pans
Searchin garbage cans
for tasty scraps
Lick my fingers clean
Of leftover
chops and bean
eyelids don't fall
spiders climb the walls
birds announce the morn
I check the lines
Hear the alarm chime
Wonder where went the time
But happy I am
Cause it aint about the money
its all about the rhymes.

Sea Wind Song

Once upon a time
in this journey through life,
I met a person,
whose words fit in my silences,
whose silences inspired my words.
I thought such a person existed not
except in my imagination.
I found her on a journey
in a steel ship with a yellow mast.
She drew my picture
sent it back to me in words
and I recognized it as my innermost thoughts caught on a sunny day
walking in a freshly plowed field
of a farm I knew only in my youth.
A red kite flew over my head
without a string
trailing a tail of twisted blue and yellow.
Meadowlarks sang as a chorus on fence posts
and tree branches
as we walked through a meadow.
She giggled and interpreted their words, speaking as they do
in a language as foreign to me
as love unrequited.
Lavender scents tinted
the sounds of her words
and i prayed that I should never wake
but my eyes were open.
Then we were on the sea
in the ship with the yellow mast.
Never did I travel so far or so fast
as we traveled those days and nights
with words taking flight.
For we left the boat
and traveled the stars and the moon
without effort
returning again to contemplate each other
and the sea.

And so it is and so it should be
that the salty sea wind
shall take me where she lives
so i may listen in silence
to her breath on a frosty crunching walk
across meadows of frozen grass.
In the night I wish most of all
to comfort her in sorrow
and share her laugh
until our voices become one
in a sea wind song
through the prairie grass.

Living Life

A plaintive sound of a train
Awakes me and my mind tells me
That yesterday I overindulged in life.
Images abound
As do the sounds
Of the people
No longer around
As I scribble these words
At two in the morning
On the day after.
A man who grew up in a small town
Who shared his story with me
After he nodded his head
When I said
I grew up as a farmer
In a small town in Nebraska
he said that was good
and that he lived in one too
when he was young
In Mexico far away.
Now we both are home in Denver

A few miles apart
Small town boys come to the city
Sharing stories of places
Known to both of us.
Mexico City, Cuernavaca and Tepostelan
When He repeated "Tepostelan"
I knew he knew the beauty
Of that small mountain town
Where the legends are handed down
About the witches gathering there
On each equinox under the moon.
And a sadness comes to my eyes
As I remember our conversation
And what I forgot to ask.
Did he know the pastorela?
The one I saw under the full moon
Outdoors on Christmas eve in Mexico City.
So by early afternoon yesterday
I had a day full of stories
Including a call from New York
From a client who needed
A contract written yesterday.
I heard disappointment
With me in his voice.
Maybe That is why I woke at 2 am
Along with all these stories.
In the afternoon yesterday
I began to finish that project
And yet another call came
It seemed the fiftieth of the day
A woman writer standing outside the building
Which houses my firm
Who told me she walked
Over the bridge and the water below
to my office
Despite her fright
of heights
Only to discover
the elevators were not working.
Her call to me on the busy day

Was plaintive like the distant train
I heard this night
and hear again and again as I write
as if it were the world
complaining of the burden
droppen like an anvil on its shoulders.
"I know I don't have an appointment" she said,
"But I came all this way
And walked across the bridge."
So we met on a bench
Overlooking the Platte River
In the cool shade of a tree
That suddenly shadowed us
On a warm October day.
Looking out over the convergence
Of the Platte and Cherry Creek
Both jumping and sparkling with unobstructed sun
She talked of her writing she wants to sell
Unread by anyone.
I sympathized
and silently wondered if I could represent everyone
that needed me or wanted me to for free.
Her voice backed by earnest brown eyes
hairnet holding silvering hair
beautifully contrasting her dark black skin
Is far different than listening
To a message on my voice mail machine.
I breathed the air, listened hard
and we talked at length
Till she gathered her things
And walked to an afternoon bus
That would take her home.
Before I trudged up the stairs to my office
I breathed deep the fall scented air.
As I stood there
a man walking on the cobble brick path
Said to me that in England people would commit suicide
If a day this gorgeous occurred
I did not understand except I agreed
That this fall day was marvelous indeed.

Finally back in my cell
Papers surrounding me,
answer a call from a friend
down from the mountains
To have a beer and talk
At a bar that is a easy walk
suddenly my vows to work all night
Dissolve into an amber light.
And so that was my story of yesterday.
What is yours?

Medals of Honor

Sounds carried on the wind,
Swirling round me,
Confounding me,
Crackling sounds of gunfire and bombs
Carried on the wind
Sent by fear and confused minds
Trapped in uniforms
Tailored for coffins
Adorned by medals of honor
Cast by oil money
Into figurines of death
Disguised as glory
By thieves of life
Burglars of youth
Manufactured by felons
Masquerading as leaders of this land
Sadly we follow
Burying the dead
Honor praised
Our Vision blinded
By the fiery blaze
Of the molten Metal
Poured into the molds
Badges of death
Medals of Honor.

Voice of the Flame

The candle lit on my table
Its flame spoke to me
"There's a flower for you
Waiting in the graveyard.
Pick up the rifle
Strap on the grenade belt."
I hesitated in the shadow of the flag
Then whispered
"God Bless America."

Dance Madly

We danced,
the rain came,
now the forcast is snow.
Struck me today that the sun warms me
The breeze cools me
life constantly fools me.
Revelations foreshadow non-occurring events
Non sequiturs abound.
I search for answers
Seemingly unfound.
So dance madly in the rain,
Before the snow comes.

Runes revealed by the moon.

Moon runes
Change
with the angle of the moon
morph
in the dark cloud shadows cast by lunar light
age
with ticks of the cosmic clock.
ever changing runes
ever beautiful rhymes
soft, bright poetry
illuminated by a single shaft of clarity.
fingerprint of a magical night
returns
only on the four hundreth day after revelation
for a moment
an instant
seen only by the vigilant
then and now.

Father

I danced alone with my father,
He on the Moon,
And me here in my room,
Until he lay on a bed almost dead,
And then we danced anew
Each of us together
For the first time we said
The name of the dance unknown to us,
I love you.

Mom

Mom you cooked me steak
On Friday afternoons before football
Listening to me rant
About winning the game
It was our little ritual.
Football ended some time ago
But you still cook me steak
And serve me at your table.
Mom you listen patiently to others
Not just me or sister or father
Nor your cool ass brothers
But those who have a desperate need
To be heard.
You listen
and offer them a friendly word
when they need it most.
Mom you always hug me
when I come home
And when I go away
In my mind each hug
seems like it happened today.

When I am away
Your letters come in the mail
Treasures of words and thought
Pictures and things I should see
Written so real
That it makes me smile
Everytime I see
Your handwriting in the mail.
Mom, in my mind
As I write these words
I hear your feet
On the steps coming to wake me
As I sleep in my bed
Upstairs at home.
I hear your voice say you love me
I smile and say I love you too.
I wish I were there.
Happy birthday from your son.

The Artist

The optic nerve twitched
And made me switch
From rum to tequila mixed.
Drinking it straight down
I Ordered another round.
Evil ways yes darling
That's how I sound.

But speed freed me from my sin
And oils splashed on the canvas again
Like a color filled rhyme
Playing all the time.

I wore only a robe
Despite the freezing cold.
The radio blared a tune
about coming too soon.
Flip the burning roach
In the trash
Paint and paper turned to ash
in an instantaneous flash.

But speed freed me from my sin
and oils splashed on the canvas again
like a color filled rhyme
Playing all the time.

Faces appeared in red
With open mouthed words
Going sadly unsaid.
Black and white,
I must be tight
The legs were long
Clearly sketched all wrong

These images just don't belong

But speed freed me from my sin
And oils splashed on the canvas again
Like a color filled rhyme
Playing all the time.

Finish with the long dark light
Of the sun dropping into night
We bleed from our days
Cut deep by the words
Of friends and fucked up foes.

But speed freed me from my sin
Oils splashed on the canvas again
Like a color filled rhyme
Playing all the time.

Yes speed freed me from my sin
Oils splashed on the canvas again
And Color filled rhymes
Played all the time.

Good nights and hellos

Good nights and hellos
Eyes close and open anew
Am I still me
Or am I you?
Bless the sleep of darkness
Yet welcome the morn
Am I still me
Or am I you?
Worlds spanned in synaptic travel
Imagination or reborn?
Am I still me
Or am I you?
I consider my hands
Curl toes inside my shoes
Am I still me
Or am I you?
Wake from the black abyss
Hearing rhymes unknown,
Am I still me
Or am I you?

Single String Guitar

Single string guitar vibrates
Through the glow of midnight harvest moon
Hanging over untrod plain of bluestem grass
Slowly swaying across pointed ears
Hidden in the foliage mass.
Man's music in animal world
Spinning a plaintive tale
Of love gained then lost
Slowly rising from the prairie
Comes a low slow howl
Universal understanding born of life
And common fate
Under the midnight harvest moon
On the untrod plain of bluestem grass.

Collection

Fresh bread sprinkled with cheese
New words twisted in poetic rhymes
Oven heat and heat from the head
tears and laughter
at my expense and on your credit.
It aint easy writing,
A perfect poem?
Impossible!
So this collection
of words will have to do.

Images of Carrol

Bicycles wheeling down gravel roads
Sweet pears tasted from his orchards
A friendly smile and a wave
From the yard where he tended his garden
A family and crops well grown
A life well lived.

On the train to Hastings

On the train to Hastings
the rails lulled me to sleep
only to wake from the deep
to Christmas Lights
wrapping a prarie courthouse
in a festive girdle drawn tight.

In the middle of summer,
On the train to Hastings
as the lights faded to white
in the middle of the night
I wondered if my waking vision
was a remembrance of the past?
Or dream of the future?

On the train to Hastings
to see my aged father
facing an operation
with lucidity and humour
in subleties and inflections
so complex they defy description.
A lesson learned only in reverie
after the fact.

On the train to Hastings
i spoke to aquaintances
left messages for friend
words crackling, barely heard
sounds fading in and out
So much we intend to say goes unknown.
cell phones provide only a hint
of the message we send
to a good friend.

On the train to Hastings
in my mind as I write
I feel the rocking cars
and see the flashing lights.
I spoke to a woman from Iowa
who did not know of the writing
of willa cather or of spoken word
but worried about the weight
of second and third graders
who cannot stop eating
or playing video games.

On the train to Hastings
my computer battery died
and i sat and talked
with a woman who flew to denver
to ride the train home
with her two daughters.

On the train to Hastings
I received messages
hints of what happened
in the world i had left
when they tore my ticket
and said take car 611
dont forget to get off
at 2:30am
we wont announce the stop

On the train to Hastings
I drank a four dollar beer
impatiently because what to do
is to find the world
hidden in the beeps and crackles
waiting for us to get off the train
so we can see the arched eyebrow refrain.

On the train to Hastings
the train lurched
and i almost fell

into a stranger's lap
but no stranger of a stranger
than the doctor who operated
on my father

On a train to Hastings
i began to realize the journey
was like my life
full of lurches and almost falls
doors to open
and doors to quickly close
a tightrope to walk
grabbing the tops of the seats
thrilled at the conclusion
of finding my seat
quite a feat
when they are all the same.

On the train to Hastings.

HEROES

Oft do I think of heroes
and wonder
Who dare stand in those shoes
In the blinding light of day?
I search for them along rivers
in courtrooms and walking city streets.
I walk wilderness trails
on tops of mountains
and in the desert sand
seeking those who
understand through action
the meaning of the word.
I stare into eyes
listen to all
who venture near
even glance into bars
and at drivers
of speeding cars.
Many a tale I hear
from those false facilitators
who fancy themselves
the boldest and the best
lawyers, actors, politicians, athletes and such.
Story telling do gooders
tattling platitudes of benign bravery
blatently begging for public adoration
in words and endless inaction.
They fashion themselves heroes,
I ridicule their pomposity
in my thoughts
as I watch them bath
in showers of golden coins
from leaders who smirk
at flimsy fakers who distract
from the bloody fact
that our youth are dying in Iraq

for oil and money.
Heroes cannot be slaves
To opinion polls
material riches
Or even adoration
By the masses.
Heroes must decide on their own
Right and wrong
Ready to stand by their decisions
As destruction descends
upon them and their battered friends.
Heroes are not made of steel
heroes are twisted and tossed aside
heroes are humiliated In the harsh public eye
heroes are abandoned by the fickle.
Death becomes a thought of escape
only for a moment because
heroes dont die
they are killed by the arrows
of popular opinion
stoned by the naive
and deceived by the rich.
All orchestrated by rulers
Scared of unflinching eyes
Facing them down
without weapons or greed.
Yes,
Heroes exist in every corridor
you will see them if you know
Ghosts who turned the corner
Knowing exactly the hell
into which they marched
Heroes who
Despite their clear vision
of impending death by friendly fire
take the trail
marked by the blood
of heroes gone before.
Heroes would say
if they understood

who they were on that fateful day
"We are one you and I,
Each day we make choices
Each day we risk our lives
Each day we own our souls."

The Imaginary Trial of George W. Bush

Old lawyer at the podium
me in the future
representing the past
old lawyer questioning a witness
who used to represent us
our former President
who sent our children to war
testifying,
answering my questions.
"Do you have blood on your fingers Sir?"
he does not reply,
for
unlike before
when he testifies in court
his writers are not there
no prompting cards next to the monitors.
I tell him the date and place of which i inquire
September 23, 2006 he asks
I had said September 25, 2006 in Iraq
but since he mentioned the 23rd
"Can you tell me what happened
in Baghdad and Iraq that day?" I ask.
"we kept the peace," he says loudly.
"Do you know Jennifer Hartman?"
No.
Do you deny she was 21 on September 23?
I don't know he said.
Isnt it true that she is now dead?
His eyes looked down
when he said i dont know.
Where was she from?
I dont know.
Do you deny she died in Iraq?
No.
Isnt it true her orders to go
came from you?
I dont know.

You are the President of the United States
The orders came from you isnt that true?
Yes.
and isnt it true that you said the reason
for all of our dead
is weapons of mass destruction
that do not exist?
I dont remember now.
Do you know Aaron Smith?
Did he die too?
He said the words to me still looking down.
The defense attorney objected saying
the question is cumulative and irrelevant.
The judge denies the objection and says
answer the question, Mr. President.
I dont think I knew him.
Would it refresh your recollection
If i said he was from Kileen Texas?
you are a texan are you not Mr. President?
Yes I am.
I still dont think I knew him.
You gave the orders that led to his death correct?
I guess so.
I was protecting our country.
You admit that you gave the order
that led to Sargeant Smith's death?
Yes.
And what was the basis for that order?
the defense attorney objected "National Security!"
the judge said "sustained" and said to me
"move on counsel."
Did you know corporal Marcus Cain before he died?
No.
With that No George W Bush cried out
Make him stop!
Make him stop!
Make him stop!

I said, move to introduce the Death report of September 23, 2006.

Defense Counsel said, Object irrelevant.
The judge said "The report shall be admitted."
As you, the jury, silently watched on
I said, "No further questions."

Memos of War

Who writes the words of war?
Or do they go unsaid?

The Souls of the persons
Writing the words of war
Drag themselves to the trashcan
On the virtual desktops
And Hit empty with crying fingers.
Souls vanish into virtual oblivion
Leaving the typists hard and cold.
Figures of ice
Tapping stiff fingers on keyboards
Covered with blood.

Who writes the words of war?
Or do they go unsaid?

Secretaries of death typing terse
Memos to the soldiers,
Order,
Today we invade Iraq,
Order,
Today we bomb the village
Near the river
Order
Today we fire the missiles
At the city bustling with civilians
Order
Today the young men
Strap on their bombs.

Who writes the words of war
Or do they go unsaid?

Follow up memos come next,
Justified by weapons of mass destruction
Be ready to censor

reports Of dead women
and their young children.
Make sure we have our
Fighters off the street
Before the missiles hit
Take credit for the destruction
Of busses of tourists
To the holy land.

Who writes the words of war?
Or do they go unsaid?

Who pushes the send button
When young men
Are blown to bloody scraps
Who keeps track on each side
Of the names of those gone
And their unborn children

Who types the words of war
Or do they go unsaid?

Do the persons who write
The words of war
Read the memos of the dead?

Who writes the words of war?
Or do they go unsaid?

Behind the Curtain

the curtain conceals the congealed
mess of the world
yet
if I pull the cord
sunlight will stream onto my wooden floor
and make a golden spot.
beyond the curtain there must be wind
and rain
not the insanity i imagine
infiltrating my closed up home.
touch the cord
feels ordinary to my hand
pull and find
those clouds above maybe
or
blood will pour from the wounded
on the streets
i forget
where am I today?
London or New York or Beirut
or home in Denver
do i dare look through the window today?

Ice Cream Over Lox

Viewers, listeners and poets
lawyers, jocks and mothers
all eating
ice cream, oil, vinegar and lox
and watching
television scenes of death
coming to unexpected recipients
living in cities not our own
sounds of crying far away from us
yet the smell of acrid smoke comes
from the pixels of the pictures
of unforseen death wrought
by unexpected soldiers.

Law and Life

Bless the law for it brought me here,
Curse the law for it brought me here,
Absolve the law for it is colorless, mindless.
I make the choices of the roads to take,
If there is blame put it at my feet.
If there is glory let me wear the wreath.
Law is my axe and my hammer
From which I have built the house
Of my life.
Tools carry no blame for murder
Nor achieve glory for stunning design
I accept the blame and the glory
That is my life.

The Lawyer Blues

I got those
Late night lawyer blues
I'm a Bleary eyed book beagle

With Scraps of coffee soaked bagels
Stewn Across the paper filled table
Head resting on the stack
Of books pulled off the rack
I Got those late nite
Lawyer blues,

Head on the table
Writing affidavits of law
and unsupported facts
Even in my sleep
I'v got those late night
Lawyer blues

Unsuspected arguments
Bubble through my brain
Until my Unkissed lips
Stop mouthing my dreams
of untraveled trips
and issues Rattle my mind

I got those late night
Lawyer blues

Grab that black and blue pen
And write those points
One to ten.
Just two more pages to read
one more date to find
then I get to sign
That I knew the answer
All the time

Yes I've got those late night
Lawyer blues
And I'm a bleary eyed book beagle.
With my head resting on the table
Hoping to buy my girlfriend
Coats of sable.

I got those late night
never lose a fight
work from dusk to dawn
Lawyer blues.

Take me to the grave
In court I will be brave

Cause I spent the time
Singing my rhymes
I got those late night
Lawyer blues.

Nova Nights

My patent attorney is an engineer
Tells me I have nothing to fear
Follow his advice and protect my company
From the pirates they are many
I laugh and cheer when he tells me the news
My patent has been approved, approved and approved
He sends me my patents, framed
So I can put them on our walls
Little did I know that if I'd make a call
To another patent attorney
Almost any one at all
The reaction to the crowding of our halls
Would be "I'm appalled."
At the sacrifice; at the enormous price;
Better to have two or three,
That pirates read and plea
For you to lower the guns and let them run
Than an armada of rowboats
None big enough to hold a gun.

A good day to you

A good day to you
The suitcoat hangs on the wall
Wrinkled from my fall
Into poverty and legal shame
Polished shoes are not the same
As a suitcoat pressed and clean.

Crossroads the Dream and the Reality

Images in our minds
Sketched the seats and the stage
From a blank space populated
Only by six concrete pillars.
Eyes Of dreamers and doers and creators
Saw tomorrow yesterday.
Dancers, actors, musicians, painters and poets
Populated our imaginary stage,
Now suddenly real and ready.
So welcome everyone
To the magical place in the center of the city.
Five Points
Where the roads and the rail meet
And creativity leaps like a dancer
Sings the blues on a Saturday nite
and tells the stories
Of this city and its people.

Thank you to everyone who helped change the dream to reality.

The Fence

Post holes dug
dirt tamped hard
blistered hands
under leather gloves
Number Nine wire spooled
steel staples in bulk
creosote posts,
big one for the corner
braces wound together
special fencing tool.
Pliers that hammer
pull,
and finally cut
wire, staples and
the dead wood rotted
at the bottom
of old hedge posts.
Pull, cut, hammer.
Pull, cut, hammer,
Pull, cut, hammer,
lines of wire hung
sweat in the eyes
breathing deep the air
swigging cold ice tea
finally
twist the smooth number nine
cut the steel
pound the last staple
watch the sun set
casting the long
fence post shadows.
Then with reluctant satisfaction,
Father and i turn
and walk home together.

Lost Yesterday

Driving my jeep,
I feel drips of warm rain
On my face.
Soft touches telling me
Drive fast to your place
Because you have the key
To the Paris
I seek to attain.
In words of delighted description,
And sketches of red, blue and black,
You give me directions
To your cul de sac.
But I,
in a gray cloud of personal distraction
fail to listen.
My look away,
As you draw only for me
Informs that I fail to see.
Sketchbook snaps shut,
Politeness paints your face,
Quick goodbye,
Hug for a stranger.
The only reminder
Of what might have been
A small tweak of my tie.
Now driving in my jeep,
Recollections of never-heard words
Turns rain
To hot torrent of tears
For one who tried to touch
My long-hidden oft-tortured soul.
What street is yours?
Where shall I turn?
No one to ask.
Cannot find my way.
Driving fast,
Not the answer for lost yesterdays.

Listen for a voice,
Imagine a touch.
Hear every word,
You do not say.
Tears and rain twist together,
Waterfalls crease my face,
Till desperation and frustration
Close my eyes
And I simply listen
For the crash
You warned about.
Instead of twisted metal screech,
I hear your voice in reprise
Lessons to me you teach.
Driving blindly,
Trusting words finally heard.
Only then,
with my eyes shut tight
do I discover
That the drops of rain
On my face
Are your tears,
From our parting embrace.

White Veils and Rice

Most know vice
Not me
Some call joy vice
Others call vice joy
Some call gay joy
Others call gay vice
Is vice simply bi?
Totally ambiguouos?
In society
Vice may be evil
Or vice may be good
Smoking cigarettes seductively
Made some rich and famous
Others miserably dead
Viceroys in hand
I consider
Vicegrips on the other hand
Pinch mercilessly if used for torture
But are tools for the unsolvable bolt
A set of adjustable wrenches
For the toolless wretch.
Ambiguous vice
Coffee, tea
Unprotected sex
Gay, straight or somewhere outside
In public?
Addiction to a mate
Is different from addiction to drugs
Vice is simple say the bankers
Robbing a bank.
But is robbing love from you
A vice of your girlfriend's new lover?
I guess vice must come down to a rendition
By someone of the seven deadly sins
Which of course I cannot remember

While I sit here smoking a cigarette
After having sex
With the wife of my next door neighbor
Vice requires thought
about those things we enjoy.
Should I have masturbated
Rather than make love with sally
Or was it Jane?
Is vice forgetting a name
In the middle of the day
Of your last born kid?
Is vice telling your mom
Something she doesn't want to hear?
Like about your divorce
Or living in sin?
Is vice dating someone
Your best friend despises?
Or is vice all in the mind?
Something we enjoy
That others say is bad?
I know what agrees with me
And that which makes my stomach turn
So I don't eat beets
But I don't tell those eating
They are flirting with vice
Unlike others
Who give their unfettered advice
When I suggest my mind
Lingers on white veils and rice.

Tears

Music carries tears in our room of words,
Tears releasing pain so we don't go insane,
Tears that cleanse our cynic's mind,
And wash away doubt of love
For all time,
Tears that bond us more than a hug,
Tears that find tears, that find tears, that find tears, that find tears
Until we smile together
And join hands in silent embrace

brass tacks

brass tacks
dirty hall
unseen words suspended
on a faded red wall
crippled old man
stops
looks left looks right
opens gnarled hand
brass tacks
scrap of paper
another poem
on faded red wall.
His door closes
a door opens
wrinkled face appears
looks left then right
then another
one by one
door by door
his words are read.

Car Wreck City

orange dawn
overflowing junk yard
dog barks echo
tipping piles of twisted metal
shading piled-high K-Mart shopping cart
yawning vagabond woke by single sun ray
through broken windshield
of his dream car never owned
a 59 corvette, silver-gray,
broken man, broken car
one by pairs of aces
the other by high speed chases
facing the new day dawn
together
at a place they call home
Car Wreck City.

Me before

I am dirt and water mixed by chubby fingers,
The wind carries sounds of red birds
happily flitting branch to branch,
Feathers float on the wing of a hawk,
I am the air around the feather,
And the feather itself.

A Ship with a Yellow Mast

I hired a ship
with a yellow mast
molten furnace ready to blast
cast onto the ocean
my shiny chrome prow
attracting flocks of ducks and geese
who provided an umbrella of sound
for my ship of steel.
Pell mell we traveled
engine and sail
destination uncertain
telling the helmsman
turn towards the sun
for this watery run.
For we sought to find
The ends of the earth
where sky meets water
and there just saunter
grin on our face
having found the place
where time stops the years
and never are there tears.
I hired a ship of steel
with a yellow mast
sailing with memory of the past
using my mind
to take me to the end of time
I laughed with the sun and moon
till together we almost swooned
now,
I travel endlessly
without a body to chain me
on the wind
cool from the deep sea rain
a wraith, a whisp, a whisper of sound
sailors often look around
silently hoping they are found

by the ship with the yellow mast
to take them homeward bound.

Survive the Night

I made it through the night
Sometimes that's quite a fight
Goblins gambled golden coins
Emboldened by the old ones
Setting odds on my survival
With each moments arrival
I made it though the night
Sometimes that's quite a fight
With the witches sly convention
Of spinning wicked wants of invention
Till I scream of my perdition
And wake once again to my condition.

Ink Stained Family

Exchange words for words
Your idea gets mine
My idea yours.
Metaphoric blood mixed
as black ink
on the same page.
And we have become
Sister and brother.
Ink Stained Family.

Vinyl Poet

I am employed by the sun,
the warm rain
and the darkest whisping clouds.
I am a poetic
hovering over the light
overlying my life
fluttering my wings
to stay here and sing.
I am the April rain
and the local city train.
I am a poetic
yes I am a poet
I am a poet of the streets
feeling the heat of the hard concrete
as I tread with my ragged feet
until I stand mute
before you on the street
where you demand respect
wearing your vivid blue suit
listening to your words
jumbled all the time
you talking over my rhymes
telling me what my words
don't say in your mind
educating me what I meant to say
without even taking the time
to listen to what i did say.
you don't understand I am a poet
and that your words I hear
so that even as i play the mime
you become an image of mine
a caricature for all time
of a person you really don't want to be.
I'm a poet
walking the streets
people talking, smells wafting
stopping to find

a person with rhythm and soul.
I'm a poet and those who know
listen to my words
don't talk over my rhymes
and when they speak
I respect them
cause they're not a fool.

Tuesday Time Lapsed Photo

Tuesday the 14th of August
I sit with the computer on my lap
rather than sudsing in the shower.
time for a black and white
scribbled photo of uncertainty
mixed with hope.
Legal work, wanna be clients,
Liens by contractors,
loans by lenders
gifts by givers
Coffee, soap and computers,
days slipping by without sentences
Lost days mean images once vivid
turn into faded old photos
nostalgic without the sharp dismay
of a stressful day.
Images out of order march
through the mind
in rebellious time.
A concrete bench and a lime ice
under a silvery russian olive tree.
Bells on the street
announcing the ice cream to all.
Then fade and materialize to a room
a wan faced man
flat on his back
tubes in his nose
and the sound of my voice
as i read.
The characters come alive
reading to my father
in a hospital room in Nebraska.
Nebraska
Nebraska

as if i had never heard the word
an Indian word.
Hills on our farm are burials
of the dead
of families living in hogans or teepees
or what did they build?
I know only the graves.
Suddenly, without warning
from my headstrong mind,
i am back with my father
and the tubes and the beeps.
A short stop and I am jerked again
Now to see
Anxious authors sheparding plays
through the theater
audiences of friends
actors of note.
I worry about loans
not what was wrote.
Listen.
Take pictures of these days,
They do not come again,
all pretense must go.
Focus i say
and the image of the pitcher
whose eye socket was broken
by a line drive so hard
he never saw it arrive
invades my conciousness
from so many years back.
yet he returned
pitching again.
Images and sounds
captured on this page.
Anger filtered out
No room for that now.
What remains is clear vision,
and intense listening
from which I paint new images
on the page.

Looking up from the words
Cats wait at my door
as if i will toss them answers
to their daily question
of what's new in your room?
they inquire briefly then dismiss
my friendly hello
with a yawn
and lick of the paw.

Forts

We searched for forts
Scattered among the trees
Built is not the right word
Rather forts of fallen trees
And dirt banks invented as ports
For wilderness wanderers
To hide from mountain lions and hawks
to observe rabbits, turkeys and deer
and to exercise imagination
of battles won and lost
through strategies of war.
I tripped on the branch
A wooden trap
Left to protect from intruders
And looked up to see my sister
Laughing so hard
She became a kid again
Exploring the woods
With her big brother
Forts built with imagination
Are always the best kind.
As we walked a deer spang away
And I shot
With my camera

Catching a bare glimpse
Of an erect white tail
I wondered at changes
Ditches of old filled in
And land walker of metal
Huge wheels and spinklers
Tend the land
As mechanized irrigators
No shovels needed
To fix gopher sabotage
On ditches of earth
We finished our walk
Back down the gravel road
In the cold
With me remembering
How many times it was ran
By me in the heat and with sweat
To arrive home again.

Reflections in the age of video

Caught on cam
No makeup on goddamn
Opposite of a pancake faced
Sweating candidate from ancient history
Richard Nixon
But all the same
Dead on unrelenting reality
Of the close up face shot
You know what I mean.
And if you say what you mean
You know it will be cut
To the version understood
By the editor on the night crew
Who is a died-in-the-wool
Punch-them-up boxing fan
Reflections in the age of video
Wink of the eye
Interpreted by all,
Differently.
Moviedom style on the 10 o clock news
equals herodom
Without takes and retakes
Or edits
Lying on the cutting room floor
Common folk get one
Come to Jesus take
And when the clapboard claps
That is it
No lunch or champagne brunch.
Branded by the camera,
Ten seconds of fame or shame
Or even unexpected blame
On the local television station.
Reflections in the age of video
Video wills spoken with venom
And vodka in hand
To the black sheep child excluded

From the family flock.
Child birth pain reinjected
Into memory
vividness uninvited
Reflections in the age of video
This video my son
Is when you were conceived
And he says
God dad that was boring sex
Reflections in the age of video
Exaggeration deflated
He was just a human
Not a hero
Stories go untold
In the face of facts.
When his well worn face
Was caught on the candid
Unexpected camera
Was he really that gorgeos?
Better to slip off screen quietly,
So you can remember the bad times better
And the good times great.

Finger Paint

Once again i dabble as i am able
with blank page flat on the table
words affixed like gobs of paint
today will i smear words with the taint
of oily grifters not saints?
Or rather shall I brush chalk
of different colors for each who talks?
Watery images make mountains sag
when their outlines I clean
with my multicolored rag.
Yes today i play with words
and paint in black and white
made colorful by my readers imagination
not sight.

Drip of water
Reminds me of rain
That cooled the summer night
Which reminds me
Of thunder clouds
On the western Nebraska skyline
Which reminds me of my youth
Standing on the pitching mound
Hearing the thunder rolling in
Which reminds me
Of a national tournament
In witchita Kansas
And gumby's dirty uniform
As he pitched
From a red-clay mound
Which reminds me
That Tidge died dead
On his kitchen floor
And that John Ropp
His Michigan twin
Is one of my best friends
I need to call
Which reminds me
That Bob Purcell published a book
Of poetry
And I should send him
Some of mine
Which reminds me
That it is past midnight
And I am sitting at a bar
Scribbling on cash register tapes
Given me by bartender
Who says bartenders are
psychiatrists not philosophers
which reminds me that sometimes
I do not understand at all
Because I am a poet.

Silent Poet

Clapping hands welcomed the departure
Of a well-loved poet
Who paused for a long moment
Before he walked off stage,
Into the anonymity of the night.
The echoes of applause
Still In his mind.
he rode an empty train.
The steel toned rhythm
Underscored words unsaid
To the hands that had clapped for him.
Pain unexpressed,
Sadness hidden,
Stories untold,
Songs unsung,
Play on the radio station
That is his ravaged mind.
Over and over
As he rides
the last train of the night
To the last stop
On a deadend line.
So clap for the silent poet
Standing on the dimly lit stage,
Alone.
Each pause saying more
Than a thousand words strung together
In rhymes played in four count time.
Truth hidden in laughter
Created by his entertaining banter.
Each of us faces death sooner or later.
Resigned, angry, sad or raging
Eyes open wide

Or eyes tightly closed
Each poet on the stage
Each person on the street
Each one of you
Face your fate
The last poem read
The last train ride.
(long pause)
so,
In the long pause of the poet
before speaking his last line
Listen to the silence.
The silence
Before the end of life
And consider
How will you finish?

Today

Today I took a picture of the misty mountains
as they turned two tones of gray
and their peaks and vales sketched themselves
on the glass canvas of my western window.

Today I wrote words that hurt
without thinking of the pain
my crooked fingers felt while scratching
shaky lines of ink.

Today I smiled at beauty,
a winsome toothy grin
and twinkling eyes.

Today i cried at stories of man and son
and laughed at my own tears
as they streamed down my twitching face

Today I traveled under skyscrapers
and through their long lanky shadows.

Today I watched tattered jean legs
stumble and lurch their unshaven face
of dark stubble and vacant eyes
Into visions reflected on water mirrors
called eyes.

Today I shared my blueberries with another
who knew
How good they are for you.

Today I received a message of hope
which tempered my message of doom
till all together the words locked
like a just found jigsaw.

Today I made keys to a dream
and printed in red
all that everyone had said
in the mists of yesterday.p

Today I said I love you
and meant it so much
it tore the lining
out of my heart.

Today I saw the evening light bath my city
and all those walking the paths in a way
that made them open their eyes
and drink the golden rays.

today draws to a close
and i feel both
the hot and the cold
the noise and the silence
the pain and the love
today today i regret all
seen and forgotten
and rejoice in the remembered.

Simple life

simple life simple things
we laud the simplification of tax forms
and jury instructions.
Yet beware
before you tear apart a friendship
due to a simple statement
stated poorly or understood badly.
Years of friendship stand
on strands of gossamer so complexly woven
that a single one defines little.
do not let,
in a single blow
that slashing steel sword of anger
sever forever the spider web of friendship
weaved delicately over the years.

Talking to Mooncows

Do mooncows live only at night?
Where do they go during the day?
Who herds mooncows in the sky?
Or are they the wild ones who escaped
Up the wire of a full moon ray?
Mooncows spy on you for fun
Disguising themselves in the dark
They never even make the dogs bark.
So how do I know they exist?
One of them tapped me on the shoulder
and told me to use their name
but not to give them any blame.
No one wants to be forgotten
a mooncow is just the same.
everyone needs some friends
So go outside tonight
And moo at the moon
Using a cow like tune.
you will hear someone say
did you have a bad day
but if you are lucky
there will be a herd
so you can say something absurd
talking to the moon
all night long.

Puddle of Dust

A puddle of dust wet on the floor
Kick the melting ice
Next to the kitchen door
Think of the missing yellow broom
With its dirt stained dust pan
And the hands that held it
In this very room.
When bending causes
twisted back muscles
To shoot excruciating
bullets of physical pain
To my sensitive brain.
That same gray mass of mine
remembers soft massages
soothing with strength and touch
till my synapses loose
the repressed recollection
of why my lost love left me.
Now gone her absence sends
Another message of pain
To my tortured brain
Kick the ice again and feel insane
As its slippery wetness spreads
Across every inch of the floor
With its crumbs of broken bread.
Bare feet coldly wetted
I pad sadly to my bed
to find That my mind
has deceived me again
because she sleeps there
waiting for me
its just that sometimes I cannot see.

Pencil Sketches

a thought of Paris in spring
dancers on the river bank
Picasso's mad paintings
shocking, mocking,
making us laugh.
partaking politely
of midnight snails
in an odd green sauce.
full moon illuminating
towers of Notre Dame
coffee and croissants
at an outdoor cafe
while observing the human array.
hunting for the perfect card
for sister and mom.
pictures of frollickers
and perfectly clad waiters.
Paris in the Spring,
stroll the banks
holding hands
spend some francs
for sketches of pencil,
now memories of yesterday
not quite put away.

Words

this evening working late
i thought of a gate
opening to a flood of words
rushing about me
swirling
covering me in ink.
as i drown i taste
the delightful nouns
with verbs rushing around
i spit out adjectives
and denounce pronouns
now i must sleep deep
in the well
where poets snuggle
with snippets of paper
scribbled with words.
such delightful nights
make my life just right.

Mind Walk

Imaginary mind walk
Through flowered fields of scribbles
Thought I had shed the blinders
Opened my eyes to day
But a dream within a dream
fooled me in my sleep.
Blue skies shed flakes of snow
Silver skinned bird waits to fly
Tanks sucking in liquid fuel
Images have no need for octane
Powered on microwaves and coffee
Shut eyed movie screen
Plays on and on,
To me alive
To others unseen.

In my dreams,
Yesterday we argued, today we fly
Yesterday we wore blue suits,
Today blue jeans.
Yesterday we learned,
today we seek.
Yesterday,
freezing Friday in Chicago,
Today,
sunny Saturday in Denver
Tomorrow,
rainy brunch in Seattle.

In my dreams,
Yesterday I farm fields of corn
Today I cruise the Seine
Tomorrow haunt the muse de orsay.
Yesterday read a book on a black sand beach,
Today sip coffe in a Marseille cafe

Tomorrow wander a flower bazaar.

Words tow a cart full of images
Ready to make themselves live
For readers imagined, and listeners real.
So open the eyes,
Scribble the words
Chant the charm,
Image arise, image alive
Image Survive!!!!!

A Writer's Dream

tonight i woke
after an hour of sleep
knowing i have little time
in which to play
with words and sentences
so this is quick
write each line
with subtle flicks
imagine the rhythm
of the beat
ta da ta da ta da.
iambic pentameter
cut two fifths short
equals three hours more
of wonderous sleep.
Tonight
the other writers
write and write and write
keeping the beat.
Good night.

tonight i woke
after an hour of sleep
knowing i have little time
in which to play
with words and sentences
so this is quick
write each line
with subtle flicks
imagine the rhythm
of the beat
ta da ta da ta da.
iambic pentameter
cut two fifths short
equals three hours more

of wonderous sleep.
Tonight
the other writers
write and write and write
keeping the beat.
Good night.

Insight to Insanity

Watching the screen
Of Televised insanity
gives me insight to vanity
Of preachers, teachers and all sorts of creatures.
Click after click, channel after channel
News of war, diamonds for sale, buffing your body
Movies galore
throw advertisements into the milieu
public broadcasting that's not for you
tits and sexy voices hyping
Toyotas, Beamers and Fords
But before you buy an Accord
grab a Big Mac and coke
and get way too fat
giving good reason to buy Nike
for the treadmill track
sitting in front of your screen
now I don't want to be mean
but at the risk of being obscene
ask yourself who is insane
those who make the money
off you and your couch bound honey?
So let me say again,
Televised insanity
gives me insight to vanity

Of preachers, teachers and all sorts of creatures.
Click after click, channel after channel
News of war, diamonds for sale, buffing your body
Movies galore
throw advertisements into the milieu
public broadcasting
Is that for you?
Stop this time
Think about this rhyme
And give a dime
To those who tell the truth.

Gritty Love

Life demands living
anything else cheats me and you.
gut wrenching walks
up 14,000 foot mountains
through snow and mud that sticks to our boots.
Challenging each others mind
until each teaches the other
lessons for all time.
We match rhyme for rhyme
day after day
month after month,
year after year.
And when you are crippled
I will carry you to the top
of that same mountain
reciting those rhymes.
And when my mind is gone
you shall cry as you teach me
the same lessons I taught you
for all time.
Gritty love,
That's all there can be this time.

Stripped

Life wraps you
In layers of emotion
Like a specially wrapped gift
That cant be opened without pain.
Life wraps you
Then strips the layers away
Sadness by death
Curiosity by fire
Love by betrayal
Hate by time
Greed by satiation
One by one stripped
Until you stand naked
In the black and white wash
Of a midnight moon
Waiting for what
You do not know.
That is the time
Our eyes will meet
And we will learn love
together from beginning to end.

Moonlit Kiss

Quiet cloaked the night
moonrays turned color into black and white
and your kiss
traveled from my lips
to my soul
and back again
translated into a whisper,
"I love you."

sharing words

Fifty may seem old
to those not here
and for youth
money may seem green
and delicious
like a crisp salad with chicken.
Before 30
arthritis impossible
parkinsons a forgotten nightmare
I ran marathons
a commercial for gatorade.
Now
a will is essential
knee brace necessary
and creations,
not sex, money or marathons define life.
Yet unchanging truth
bridges the chasm of time
separating youth from age.
Friends,
friends who listen
friends who laugh, cry
and comfort one another
in dark moments.
creations mean nothing
if not shared.
Thus i share with you
the chaos that is my mind.
I hope and know
that from swirling chaos
comes creativity
magic meant to make you
laugh and cry.
And I will comfort you

in your darkest hour,
even when i vanish.
Just as now i look upon my shelves for a friend
whose words
reveal that another
traveled my road

Memory Quilt

Sarah left a few minutes ago. Before she left I showed her the memory quilt that my mother had given me in 1993. Actually my mom and dad gave it to me for Christmas in 1993. I gave Sarah of the card that my mom had written to me and had her read it to me. She read, "Kurt, December 1993. This is a 'memory quilt'. Several of the blocks come from pants you wore to high school. The ideas came from Dad and I and Dianne. Sean colored in the corn-Pat and Callie approved the design. Love, dad and mom." When Sarah finished reading the card she said, "That is wonderful. Maybe they can be my mom and dad too."

Sunlight and Shadows

Sunlight and shadows in an empty broken down house on a dirt country road. Sit in the doorway and watch for movement in the shadow by the wall. Scared a bit you laugh and talk out loud even though there's no one around. "Hello" you say. "Hello there." No one answers or was the creaking of the boards in the winds an answer to your "Hello" in a strange other language. Can you stay sitting in that doorway listening to the music of the old house on the dirt country road where long ago a woman lived with a boy just your age? You wonder for a moment if she still lives here with her son, but you shake your head and softly sing to yourself,

I sit here just like you did
watching those shadows you saw
as the sun goes down.
the light gets thicker and thicker
so that I can taste the golden day.
please come whisper in my ear
if you sat right here on this doorstep
waiting for the sunset.
Then you are quiet and, when the wind whispers to you, tears fall from your eyes as the sun slips below the horizon.

The End